LISTEN MORE AND TALK LESS

RONNIE FOX

PUBLISHING

Scripture quotations marked NLT are taken from the New Living Translation®, Copyright © 1996, 2004, and 2015. Used by permission of Tyndale House Publishers, a Division of Tyndale House Ministries. All rights reserved.

Scripture quotations marked HCSB are taken from the Holman Christian Standard Bible®, Copyright © 1999, 2000, 2002, 2003, 2009 by Holman Bible Publishers. Used by permission. Holman Christian Standard Bible®, Holman CSB®, and HCSB® are federally registered trademarks of Holman Bible Publishers.

ISBN Paperback: 978-1-940449-24-1

ISBN eBook: BO8NMW9X6F

BeyondMyStrength.com

FOREWORD

God wants a personal connection with every person. The Bible tells us He created us in His own image ...

> "So God created human beings in his own image.
> In the image of God he created them;
> male and female he created them."
> (*Genesis 1:27 NLT*)

A conversation with God is amazing. The creator of the universe really wants to talk with you. It is actually His idea.

Mankind is unique in all of creation. An integral part of being human is the capacity to have a relationship. We were created as relational beings as a reflection of God's image.

A relationship with God may sound anything but simple. We don't bring anything of value. God is nothing like us. If we focus on the differences, a personal relationship with Him seems impossible. But remember, Jesus said,

> "Jesus looked at them intently and said,
> 'Humanly speaking, it is impossible.
> But with God everything is possible.'"

(*Matthew 19:26 NLT*)

The Bible is full of examples of God taking the initiative in His relationship with individuals. He spoke directly to people throughout the Bible.

Since He desires a genuine relationship, it is free of coercion. It is logical. He created mankind with the freedom to reject Him. You make the choice. God wouldn't have it any other way.

Therein lies the miracle. God created you with the unique ability to relate to him on a personal level. God does not want a relationship with you because of your IQ. It is not because you behave better than the next person.

He created you as a unique individual. Your individuality is what He wants, not your intellectual capacity.

Relationship is about companionship. The words used by a dictionary to define "companionship" include "friendship, fellowship, closeness, togetherness, intimacy, rapport, and brotherhood."

Note this description of Jesus in the Bible: "The Son of Man (Jesus) has come eating and drinking, and you say, 'Look, a glutton and a drunkard, a friend of tax collectors and sinners!'" (*Luke 7:34 HCSB*) Take care not to allow the context to obscure the fact that Jesus is described as "a friend."

He does not get bored with you because you need to sleep. He does not take offense when you get distracted. He loves you the way you are. He is patient when you let life get in the way, and is always ready to welcome you back. He understands you even better than you understand yourself.

In short, He wants to be your friend.

INTRODUCTION

The secret to a deeper relationship with God is to listen more and talk less. That is the objective of this guide.

The title "Prayer Journaling" is used loosely. This phrase is often used to describe the combination of traditional journaling, writing down one's thoughts, with prayer. This guide is an expansion of that concept. Before one prays, before one talks to God, this method guides users to listen to God, and then respond to what He says.

What you write, what you say to God, should be your response to what you hear Him say. It is about a conversation. The topic each day should be directed by God (not even this guide). The objective is not to focus on what you want to talk about; instead, let God direct the subject matter.

A seven week design provides enough days to practice listening to God and consequently develop a habit. The key is to learn what works for you. God created us and understands that each person is different.

This step by step guide is not intended to be followed without change. It is a track to run on while you practice listening to

God. Don't be afraid to experiment. By the end of seven weeks you will discover what works best for you.

The version of the Bible or even the language is not the most important element. Listening to God is the objective. The use of multiple English translations to better understand and hear God speak is a good practice. A Bible app can give you access to several different translations without any cost to you.

Spanish is a second language for me. As a missionary in Peru, I became fluent in the language of the people I was called to reach. Hearing God speak in Spanish was a valuable part of my language learning and especially my preparation to preach in Spanish. Hearing God's voice in another language helped me listen with a different focus. Sometimes a dictionary helped me have a better understanding, even in English.

The following pages are intended as a guide. Do not limit God to the outline. Follow His lead. He may lead you to expand a day to include other parts of the Bible. He may bring something to mind, even a fragment of a verse. As God redirects, follow His lead.

Listening to God will probably take you to places that may surprise you. God has something personal to say to you and it is worth your time. There may be moments when God reminds you of a verse or verses from the Bible. Find them and read them again. (Bible apps and even old fashion reference books can help you search.) God may show you something you have never seen before.

The length of your time with God will likely vary. As long as you keep the focus on hearing God speak, the amount of time really does not matter. What you get out of a relationship is usually in direct proportion to what you put in. Don't hesitate to invest more of yourself in the relationship.

HOW TO USE THIS GUIDE

The primary objective of this guide is to listen to God more and talk less.

God speaks through the Bible. It is the most reliable way to hear Him speak. Focus on what He has to say. If you are task oriented, or if you like checking the box when you're done, be careful. This is about a relationship, not about checking a box.

A simple format is designed to assist users to focus on listening to God. Each day begins with a brief introduction designed to provide a general heading.

The suggested reading assignment from the Bible is the part where God speaks. A chapter or some verses are suggested, but God may take you in a different direction. He may even take you to additional verses in the Bible.

There is no right or wrong response. Matter of fact, what you write may be brief or even cryptic. Each day has a section where you make notes about what God is saying. Be concise. You might even use a list or a few key words.

Your writing is a prayer. It is what you want to say to God in response to what you heard Him say. Set aside your want list and talk to God. What you write will likely be only a summary of a longer conversation.

Remember: The objective is to listen to God more and talk less.

PART ONE
WEEK 1

INTRODUCTION TO FIRST WEEK

Listening to God is life changing. His objective is a conversation. He wants you to hear His voice and He wants to listen to yours.

Dialogue changes everything. God speaks to you right where you are. He knows your emotions, your secrets, your good and bad qualities, your hopes and dreams, your pain and disappointments. God really understands you better than anyone, even better than you.

The amazing thing is He loves us even though we had rejected Him. God explains, even though you were against me, like an enemy, I did what was needed to make it right between us. I love you so much that even when you were against me, Jesus died in your place. He paid the debt you owed. All you have to do is accept it. (*Romans 5:8-11*)

The words of the first verse of the old song *Amazing Grace* capture my response.

> Amazing grace, How sweet the sound
> That saved a wretch like me.
> I once was lost, but now I am found,
> Was blind, but now I see.

God hears my words and knows what I really need to say. Even when I borrow beautiful words like these, I have an interpreter.

He reminds me in the Bible, I don't even know what God wants me to ask for or to say. He tells me, the Holy Spirit knows. He asks with a type of groaning that cannot be expressed with words. (*Romans 8:26*)

He wants a conversation with me. He wants me to understand.

Jesus, who is God, says, he has unlimited power everywhere. (*Matthew 28:18*)

Then He gives us an assignment, everywhere we go, we are to invite people of every type to follow Jesus. We are to baptize these followers by the power of God the Father - the Living God - creator of everything. Baptize these new followers, in the powerful name of Jesus, and in the name of God the Holy Spirit - who lives in those who choose to follow Jesus. (*Matthew 28:19*)

There is more to His assignment. We are to teach them to do all that Jesus teaches. (*Matthew 28:20*)

He ends with a reminder not to forget, Jesus is always with us. (*Matthew 28:20*)

Each follower of Jesus has the same assignment. We all have access to the same power, the same message to deliver, and the same responsibility to keep passing it along.

A relationship with God grows stronger with regular conversation. The focus of this guide is to practice talking less and listening more.

For decades, my devotional time centered on what I wanted. I called it my prayer list. My time with God was dominated by a list of my requests. Sometimes it was a long list of things I wanted. Other times it was divided into major topics for each day of the week. The theme was the same. My prayer time was all about what I wanted God to do for me and the people I cared about.

Asking God for something is not bad or wrong. He is a loving father and enjoys giving good things to his children.

As a father, my relationship with my children would be very different if I only heard from them when they wanted something. Don't misunderstand, dads love to give good things to their children. However, I really love it when we just talk. My relationship with them is deeper and richer because we talk. They invite me into their lives. I hear about their hopes and dreams. We have a relationship built on the time we spend talking and listening.

I want that with my Heavenly Father. To achieve it, I needed to get away from my selfishness and learn to listen to God. Our time together needed to be more than my want list.

A conversation with God required me to be a better listener. I called it "prayer journaling", but a better name might be a "conversation record."

The methodology is not entirely mine, but I do not know where to give the credit. The drive behind my thinking can be summed up in a single statement: *talk less and listen more.*

Based on these two simple objectives, I started a personal devotion plan in October of 1995. We were on stateside assignment as missionaries assigned to Peru. I had been in full time ministry since graduating from seminary 15 years before.

The new plan was simple.

- I recorded the date and Scripture reference.
- I listened to God.
- I wrote my response.

Listening to God was listening to the Bible. God spoke to me clearly and daily as I read the Bible or listened to it on CDs or later on my Bible app. Then I wrote a few sentences as my response to what God had said to me. It was my prayer, thus the title "prayer journal."

My written prayer often gave clues to what God had said, but unfortunately, I was not intentional about recording God's side of the conversation. What was clear was the part of the Bible I read for that day. The ratio was important. Since my objective was to listen more and talk less, my writing reflected that commitment.

In 2017 I read each of those one thousand nine hundred eighty six entries. They were not profound writings. The words I wrote would probably not be interesting to anyone else. What I discovered was how God was working in my life. It should not surprise anyone, but my family faced some of the most difficult tests we had ever encountered during those days. God's timing was amazing.

An important fact surfaced during my review. In those entries were five and a half years of hearing from God. Why? Because I chose to listen.

I do not promise that your life will or will not be easier if you follow this plan. What I know now is God used it to speak to me during many difficult periods of my life. He knew what I needed even before those challenges came.

WEEK 1 DAY 1

The focus of this first day is God. He speaks. Listening to Him begins by understanding that He wants to talk to you. It is His idea.

Hear God speak:
Psalm 50

"Listen, My people, and I will speak; I will testify against you, Israel. I am God, your God." (*Psalms 50:7 HCSB*)

My Conversation with God:

_____

_____

_____

_____

_____

_____

_____

God created everything. The first chapter of Genesis describes each part of creation with a simple phrase: "Then God said." Eight separate times, the same phrase is used. It may be translated into different English words, but the meaning is unmistakable. There is power in what God says.

Hear God speak:
Genesis 1

"Then God said ..." (*Genesis 1:3, 6, 9, 11, 14, 20, 24, 26 HCSB*)

My Conversation with God:

_____

_____

_____

_____

_____

_____

_____

WEEK 1 DAY 3

The voice of the Lord is powerful. Psalm 29 ends with an amazing declaration; "The Lord gives His people strength; the Lord blesses His people with peace." It is personal. A relationship with God is an intimate relationship with the creator of the universe.

Hear God speak:
Psalms 29

"The voice of the Lord is above the waters. The God of glory thunders — the Lord, above vast waters, the voice of the Lord in power, the voice of the Lord in splendor." (*Psalms 29:3-4 HCSB*)

My Conversation with God:

_____

_____

_____

_____

_____

Christians are often so focused on how God speaks that we miss what He is saying. God did not speak in the wind (v. 11), He did not speak in the earthquake (v.11), and He did not speak in the fire (v. 12). God spoke in a soft whisper (v. 12).

Hear God speak:
1 Kings 19

"When Elijah heard it, he wrapped his face in his mantle and went out and stood at the entrance of the cave. Suddenly, a voice came to him and said ...'" (*1 Kings 19:13 HCSB*)

My Conversation with God:

_____

_____

_____

_____

_____

_____

Hearing God speak out loud is as simple as reading the Bible out loud or listening to it on a Bible app. The words of the Bible are God speaking. It is reliable. Some make a mistake and get hung up on the relatively unimportant things like the version or language translation and miss the chance to hear God's voice.

Hear God speak:
Mark 1

"And a voice came from heaven: You are My beloved Son; I take delight in You!" (*Mark 1:11 HCSB*)

My Conversation with God:

_____

_____

_____

_____

_____

WEEK 1 DAY 6

Psalm 119 is the longest chapter in the Bible. It is entirely dedicated to the greatness of God's Word. It describes it as "instruction", "decrees", "precepts", "statutes", commands", and so much more.

Hear God speak:
Psalms 119

"I have treasured Your word in my heart so that I may not sin against You." (*Psalm 119:11 HCSB*)

"Your word is a lamp for my feet and a light on my path." (*Psalms 119:105 HCSB*)

My Conversation with God:

_____

_____

_____

_____

_____

When Jesus was asked, "What is the greatest commandment?" He quoted a verse that every Jew would know. The question is, does this express your thoughts?

Hear God speak:
Matthew 22 and Deuteronomy 6

"He said to him, 'Love the Lord your God with all your heart, with all your soul, and with all your mind. This is the greatest and most important command.'" (*Matthew 22:37-38 HCSB*)

"Listen, Israel: The Lord our God, the Lord is One. Love the Lord your God with all your heart, with all your soul, and with all your strength." (*Deuteronomy 6:4-5 HCSB*)

My Conversation with God:

_____

_____

_____

_____

PART TWO
WEEK 2

INTRODUCTION TO SECOND WEEK

The first step to a relationship with God is knowing and admitting He exists. Hoping He is real is not enough. A "just in case" or "covering all the bases" attitude is not a solid foundation.

Depth in any relationship comes from time spent together. Shared experiences are the building blocks.

God takes the initiative, but a relationship requires at least two. A response from you is an essential ingredient.

A friendship or relationship with God is planted or founded on something real. Then you build on the foundation through spending time together. Your one-on-one conversation with Him is the key.

He knows everything about you. It is impossible to hide anything from Him. He already knows the good and the bad. You can rest in the knowledge that He loves you even though He is aware of every bad thing you've done.

Letting your disobedience stand between you and God hinders your relationship. It's like the elephant in the room. You both know it's there. That's why confession is important. It is not to beat you down, it is to remove any hindrance.

God does not expect perfection from you. Instead, He provides forgiveness. What He wants is a personal relationship with you, and as remarkable as that sounds, it's true.

It is amazing to comprehend that the creator of everything wants a relationship with you. His desire is something we cannot fully understand. Even King David, a man after God's own heart, has difficulty wrapping his head around this astounding truth. He says, "... what is man that You remember him, the son of man that You look after him?" (*Psalms 8:4 HCSB*)

Relax and enjoy getting to know Him.

WEEK 2 DAY 1

A vital first step in a relationship with God is the belief that He really exists. There is an element of faith involved. Evidence of God is everywhere in creation. But faith is still necessary.

Hear God speak:
Psalm 139

"Lord, You have searched me and known me." (*Psalms 139:1 HCSB*)

My Conversation with God:

_____

_____

_____

_____

_____

_____

_____

WEEK 2 DAY 2

David wrote a Psalm to express his marvel that God would even give a thought to man. He gives examples of God's greatness. Yet, he wonders why. The Psalm ends with a declaration that captures both his amazement and his thankfulness, "Joyful indeed are those whose God is the Lord."

Hear God speak:
Psalm 144

"O Lord, what are human beings that you should notice them, mere mortals that you should think about them?" (*Psalms 144:3 NLT*)

My Conversation with God:

_____

_____

_____

_____

_____

WEEK 2 DAY 3

God provided a way to allow us to have a right relationship with Him. Jesus died in our place. Our sin separates us from God, but He paid to take it away.

Hear God speak:
Romans 5

"But God showed his great love for us by sending Christ to die for us while we were still sinners." (*Romans 5:8 NLT*)

My Conversation with God:

_____

_____

_____

_____

_____

_____

_____

People are often confused and mistakenly think they reach out to God. The truth is, He reaches out to redeem us. He paid a great price to buy us back.

Hear God speak:
1 Peter 2

"But you are not like that, for you are a chosen people. You are royal priests, a holy nation, God's very own possession. As a result, you can show others the goodness of God, for he called you out of the darkness into his wonderful light." (*1 Peter 2:9 NLT*)

My Conversation with God:

_____

_____

_____

_____

_____

_____

WEEK 2 DAY 5

The focus of this prayer guide is to talk less and listen more. Many prayer plans focus on what we say to God. They often degenerate into a want list. Although God desires us to ask Him for what we need, He is interested in a two way conversation. He has a lot to say; if we listen.

Hear God speak:
Proverbs 18

"The one who gives an answer before he listens — this is foolishness and disgrace for him." (*Proverbs 18:13 HCSB*)

My Conversation with God:

_____

_____

_____

_____

_____

_____

WEEK 2 DAY 6

The Bible reminds us to be quick to hear and slow to speak. This concept demonstrates the priority of listening compared to talking. Hearing God should precede action.

Hear God speak:
James 1

"Understand this, my dear brothers and sisters: You must all be quick to listen, slow to speak, and slow to get angry." (*James 1:19 NLT*)

"But don't just listen to God's word. You must do what it says. Otherwise, you are only fooling yourselves." (*James 1:22 NLT*)

My Conversation with God:

_____

_____

_____

_____

In Nehemiah, the Bible touched the heart of those who heard it and listened to it. They acted on what they heard. They were motivated to do something.

Hear God speak:
Nehemiah 8

"They read out of the book of the law of God, translating and giving the meaning so that the people could understand what was read." (*Nehemiah 8:8 HCSB*)

My Conversation with God:

_____

_____

_____

_____

_____

_____

_____

PART THREE
WEEK 3

INTRODUCTION TO THIRD WEEK

God is known as our Heavenly Father. He is a good father. Actually, He is a perfect father.

"Our Father in heaven" is how Jesus taught us to talk to God in what we call the Lord's Prayer. This is just a model. It is not magic words designed to be quoted from memory.

It does give us insight into how a relationship with God works. Jesus teaches us to begin with a recognition of the unique relationship every follower has with God. We are to see God as our "Heavenly Father."

This is good news for everyone, but even more precious for anyone who has not had a good earthly father. If your earthly father has hurt you, left you, or even died before you really knew him, a relationship with your Heavenly Father replaces hurt, pain, and even abandonment with His tenderness and love.

Earthly fathers are not perfect. There are some fathers who treat their children well. They want the best for their children. On the other end of the spectrum are those who mistreat and endanger their children. Even the best earthly father can't measure up to the kind of father God is.

God corrects His children through disciplines. He truly loves them and wants the best for them. Genuine love motivates a parent to correct their child.

Dispensing correction requires effort. It really can be painful for the parent. It is usually easier on the parent, especially in the short term, to let bad behavior go unpunished.

However, God loves us so much that He deals proactively with our behavior problems. He views many of our hardships as a way to help us improve. No, it is not comfortable, but God uses them as teachable moments.

Testing is not a proving ground for faith, it was an opportunity for God to demonstrate His powerful faithfulness. The strength or ability to overcome is not the main objective. Severe testing forces us to admit we need help. That's when God can really do His best work.

Too often we think God wants us to mature and overcome. What He really wants us to understand is that we need Him. Challenging times do not provide a chance to prove our ability to succeed, it is the proof that we cannot do it without God.

A relationship with God is in part an expression of our need. Our partnership with the creator is so much more, yet learning to trust Him is part of the foundation.

WEEK 3 DAY 1

God is the creator. He made everything. Real joy comes from knowing Him and trusting Him. He alone is worthy of all our confidence. He is the source of our singing, our rejoicing, and our praise.

Hear God speak:
Psalm 33

"For the word of the Lord is right, and all His work is trustworthy." (*Psalms 33:4 HCSB*)

My Conversation with God:

_____

_____

_____

_____

_____

_____

_____

WEEK 3 DAY 2

The love of God, as our loving Heavenly Father, is expressed in His willingness to walk us through difficult times. His discipline is evidence of kinship to Him as our Father.

Hear God speak:
Psalm 118
Hebrews 12

"The Lord disciplined me severely but did not give me over to death." (*Psalms 118:18 HCSB*)

"Endure suffering as discipline: God is dealing with you as sons. For what son is there that a father does not discipline?" (*Hebrews 12:7 HCSB*)

My Conversation with God:

_____

_____

_____

_____

God does not promise to rescue us from every difficult situation. His promise is to use everything, good or bad, to accomplish His purpose.

Hear God speak:
Romans 8

"We know that all things work together for the good of those who love God: those who are called according to His purpose." (*Romans 8:28 HCSB*)

Don't let the word "predestined" in verse 29 confuse you. The verse says "those He foreknew He predestined ..." That simply means He guaranteed what He knew ahead of time would happen. God is not bound by time. Therefore, He knows the future like it has already happened.

My Conversation with God:

_____

_____

_____

WEEK 3 DAY 4

Genuine faith always leads to doing something. Faith naturally leads to action. Stated another way, if faith is authentic, actions will follow. (Note: Doing good things does not save you, it doesn't even help. However, doing good things is the evidence you really have changed.)

Hear God speak:
James 2

"What good is it, dear brothers and sisters, if you say you have faith but don't show it by your actions? Can that kind of faith save anyone?" (*James 2:14 NLT*)

My Conversation with God:

_____

_____

_____

_____

_____

Jonah ran from God and from his assigned task. Even after he did what God asked, he was mad at God. Trust requires more than just doing an assignment, it involves the correct attitude.

Hear God speak:
Jonah 1 - Jonah 4
(The book of Jonah)

"This change of plans greatly upset Jonah, and he became very angry. So he complained to the Lord about it: 'Didn't I say before I left home that you would do this, Lord? That is why I ran away to Tarshish! I knew that you are a merciful and compassionate God, slow to get angry and filled with unfailing love. You are eager to turn back from destroying people. Just kill me now, Lord! I'd rather be dead than alive if what I predicted will not happen.'" (*Jonah 4:1-3 NLT*)

My Conversation with God:

_____

_____

_____

Faith results in action without knowing or understanding. Faith does not mean we understand it all. There is no promise that we will one day understand.

Hear God speak:
Hebrews 11

"Now faith is the reality of what is hoped for, the proof of what is not seen." (*Hebrews 11:1 HCSB*)

My Conversation with God:

_____

_____

_____

_____

_____

_____

_____

Real faith is believing and yet knowing that's not enough. It is understanding that what I can do in faith is limited. God can and does make up the difference. He is willing to make up for what I lack.

Hear God speak:
Mark 9

"Immediately the father of the boy cried out, 'I do believe! Help my unbelief.'" (*Mark 9:24 HCSB*)

My Conversation with God:

_____

_____

_____

_____

_____

_____

_____

PART FOUR
WEEK 4

INTRODUCTION TO FOURTH WEEK

God is what it's all about. Unfortunately, He is often given less credit than He deserves.

Projectionism is when an individual projects their own internal beliefs or perceptions on someone else. As a human being, I tend to think God sees life the same way I do.

However, God is not like me. He thinks differently. He acts differently. God speaks to this in the Bible when He says, "'For My thoughts are not your thoughts, and your ways are not My ways.' This is the Lord's declaration. 'For as heaven is higher than earth, so My ways are higher than your ways, and My thoughts than your thoughts.'" (*Isaiah 55:8-9 HCSB*)

There is really very little similarity between God and people. The amazing truth is God is for me. He does not let our differences become a barrier.

Jesus is God. That in itself is beyond my capacity to comprehend. I cannot explain God. I am actually okay with that. I would not respect God if I found Him easy to understand and explain.

The Trinity is something I simply accept. There are ways to describe it, but they are not comprehensive. God is the Father, the Son, and the Holy Spirit. Three in one. I know that and accept it as fact, but I can't explain it very well.

God is life. God is love. Let's face it, God is indescribable.

Words are inadequate.

Loving God shows in my obedience. Jesus says, "If you love Me, you will keep My commands." (*John 14:15 HCSB*) The best way to show respect and love is to do what He says.

If you have God, you have everything. That may be simplistic but it's true. God is all I need.

WEEK 4 DAY 1

I find it easy to attribute my motives to God. Unfortunately, it is usually not accurate. God is not like me and He does not think like me.

Hear God speak:
Isaiah 46
Jeremiah 10

"Remember the things I have done in the past. For I alone am God! I am God, and there is none like me." (*Isaiah 46:9 NLT*)

"Lord, there is no one like you! For you are great, and your name is full of power." (*Jeremiah 10:6 NLT*)

My Conversation with God:

_____

_____

_____

_____

_____

God is on our side. However, we are not perfect. That is one reason Jesus reminds us what the greatest commandment is, "... Love the Lord your God with all your heart, with all your soul, and with all your mind. This is the greatest and most important command." (Matthew 22:37-38 HCSB)

Hear God speak:
Psalm 56

"My enemies will retreat when I call to you for help. This I know: God is on my side! I praise God for what he has promised; yes, I praise the Lord for what he has promised." (*Psalms 56:9-10 NLT*)

My Conversation with God:

_____

_____

_____

_____

_____

WEEK 4 DAY 3

In the first chapter of John, the Word is another name for Jesus. He is God and He has always existed. He created the world and holds it together. God, in Jesus, limited Himself in order to live in the world He created.

Hear God speak:
John 1

"In the beginning the Word already existed. The Word was with God, and the Word was God. He existed in the beginning with God. God created everything through him, and nothing was created except through him." (*John 1:1-3 NLT*)

"So the Word became human and made his home among us. He was full of unfailing love and faithfulness. And we have seen his glory, the glory of the Father's one and only Son." (*John 1:14 NLT*)

My Conversation with God:

_____

_____

WEEK 4 DAY 4

God sustains my life. After feeding 5,000 people, Jesus made a powerful statement declaring, "I am the bread of life." He is the nourishment we need. When life seems hard, when our world seems to be falling apart, God is everything we really need.

Hear God speak:
John 6
Psalm 54

"I am the bread of life." (*John 6:48 HCSB*)

"The Spirit alone gives eternal life. Human effort accomplishes nothing. And the very words I have spoken to you are spirit and life." (*John 6:63 NLT*)

"God is my helper; the Lord is the sustainer of my life." (*Psalms 54:4 HCSB*)

My Conversation with God:

_____

_____

Some people place a high value on the things they have or want. Yet, God is more valuable than anything.

Hear God speak:
Psalm 20
Psalm 34

"Some nations boast of their chariots and horses, but we boast in the name of the Lord our God." (*Psalms 20:7 NLT*)

"You who are His holy ones, fear Yahweh, for those who fear Him lack nothing." (*Psalms 34:9 HCSB*)

My Conversation with God:

_____

_____

_____

_____

_____

_____

PART FIVE
WEEK 5

INTRODUCTION TO FIFTH WEEK

Faith is not a set of rules to follow. A frequent misunderstanding about faith in God is that it can be summed up in a set of rules. The Ten Commandments are often offered as evidence. But faith is about a relationship.

God does not desire great acts of faith. His top priority is a personal relationship. It is what He wants most. He is not impressed by great acts of sacrifice and devotion. Matter of fact, He can do anything with our smallest amount of faith.

Expecting blessings is not a proper motivation. We love God because He first loves us. But it is impossible and improper to ignore the benefits. We also realize that following the example of Jesus leads us to sacrifice. We are reminded to "count the cost".

The Bible invites us to imitate God. Our greatest gift to Him is a deep desire to be like Him and act like Him. He wants us to be His disciples, His followers. We honor Him when we strive to be like Him. It is impossible to succeed in our own power. He wants us to willingly put our wants to death in order to truly live by His power.

Generosity is part of our imitation of God. He is a giver. Being like Him means being generous. We see it in our personal belongings. Our stuff is less precious and giving stuff away becomes easier. We learn to give because it is truly "more blessed to give than to receive."

Imitating God also drives the motivation we have to pass on what we receive from Him. Giving away what we are learning is certainly a major part. Every follower of Jesus is expected to pass along what has been entrusted to him. We are not a container God pours into. Instead, we allow God's blessings to flow through us and bless other people as He blesses us.

WEEK 5 DAY 1

Hearing about Jesus gives birth to genuine faith. Jesus is the only way to restore a relationship with God.

Hear God speak:
Romans 10

"So faith comes from what is heard, and what is heard comes through the message about Christ." (*Romans 10:17 HCSB*)

My Conversation with God:

_____

_____

_____

_____

_____

_____

_____

_____

The law is a set of rules and only demonstrates our inability to live a perfect life. Faith is not living up to that standard. It is impossible. Faith is recognizing we can't, and placing our trust in Jesus.

Hear God speak:
Romans 3

"For no one can ever be made right with God by doing what the law commands. The law simply shows us how sinful we are. But now God has shown us a way to be made right with him without keeping the requirements of the law, as was promised in the writings of Moses and the prophets long ago. We are made right with God by placing our faith in Jesus Christ. And this is true for everyone who believes, no matter who we are." (*Romans 3:20-22 NLT*)

My Conversation with God:

_____

_____

_____

WEEK 5 DAY 3

The size of your faith is not important. The power of God, the one you have faith in, is what counts. Faith in God is faith in the one with unlimited power.

Hear God speak:
Matthew 17
Luke 17

"'Because of your little faith,' He told them. 'For I assure you: If you have faith the size of a mustard seed, you will tell this mountain, "Move from here to there," and it will move. Nothing will be impossible for you." (*Matthew 17:20 HCSB*)

"The apostles said to the Lord, 'Show us how to increase our faith.' The Lord answered, 'If you had faith even as small as a mustard seed, you could say to this mulberry tree, "May you be uprooted and be planted in the sea," and it would obey you!'" (*Luke 17:5-6 NLT*)

My Conversation with God:

_____

_____

Our desire to imitate God flows from our desire to be like Him. The natural human drives must be abandoned. We do not naturally respond like God.

Hear God speak:
Ephesians 5

"Therefore, be imitators of God, as dearly loved children." (*Ephesians 5:1 HCSB*)

My Conversation with God:

_____

_____

_____

_____

_____

_____

_____

God does not teach you things for you alone. He expects you to pass it on to others who will pass it on to still others. He does not want you to horde it. Notice the forward look Paul describes as he thinks about the ones Timothy will teach passing on what they learn. Paul sees far beyond the person he is teaching.

Hear God speak:
2 Timothy 2

"You have heard me teach things that have been confirmed by many reliable witnesses. Now teach these truths to other trustworthy people who will be able to pass them on to others." (*2 Timothy 2:2 NLT*)

My Conversation with God:

_____

_____

_____

_____

WEEK 5 DAY 6

It sounds backwards. Hardship or struggle is actually good for you. It does not make you stronger, instead it proves you cannot do it by yourself. Let God do it for you. That is His way. Difficulties are not an opportunity to prove you can, they are a time to build a dependance on God.

Hear God speak:
1 Peter 4

"Dear friends, don't be surprised at the fiery trials you are going through, as if something strange were happening to you." (*1 Peter 4:12 NLT*)

My Conversation with God:

_____

_____

_____

_____

_____

WEEK 5 DAY 7

The benefits of obedience are a long life and well-being. Cause and effect are at work. Remembering God's teachings. Living by them equals a great life and eternal life.

Hear God speak:
Proverbs 3

"My child, never forget the things I have taught you. Store my commands in your heart. If you do this, you will live many years, and your life will be satisfying." (*Proverbs 3:1-2 NLT*)

My Conversation with God:

_____

_____

_____

_____

_____

_____

PART SIX

WEEK 6

INTRODUCTION TO SIXTH WEEK

Jesus is there to help you succeed. The first step of faith is the very reason He came. Jesus is God's way to restore our relationship with Him.

Jesus came to earth to save us. God uses words like "redeem", "restore", "salvation", and "substitution" to describe the purpose for which Jesus came to earth and eventually died on a cross.

The victory came when He rose from the dead. Jesus conquered death and the grave. Death is the one thing that is universally feared by humanity. Jesus came to take that threat away.

We have a vital part in God's plan. It is our commission to tell everyone that Jesus is the answer. We are to give testimony to the change in our life.

Paul gave us a simple example of how to tell someone about Jesus. He simply told about his life before he met Jesus. Then he explained how he met Jesus. He used simple terms to tell how he became a follower of Jesus. Then he concluded with the way his life had changed. Any follower of Jesus can do the same.

We are not left in the dark. We have one of Jesus' sermons to instruct us. His teaching covers everything we need to know. Jesus used everyday examples called parables to help us learn.

Jesus died on a cross. His purpose can be summed up in His selfless act.

His death on a cross was vitally important, but His resurrection is the real victory. We follow Him as a risen Savior.

Theologically, it is probably more accurate to say we have the Holy Spirit living in us. But since Jesus and the Holy Spirit are both God that is getting in deeper than necessary for this guide. Simply stated, the hope of glory is Jesus in you.

Hear God speak:
Colossians 1

"For God wanted them to know that the riches and glory of Christ are for you Gentiles, too. And this is the secret: Christ lives in you. This gives you assurance of sharing his glory." (*Colossians 1:27 NLT*)

My Conversation with God:

_____

_____

_____

_____

_____

Jesus came for one reason. He came to save sinners. The salvation He provides makes a relationship with God possible.

Paul points out that he considered himself the worst sinner. It is not a contest to see who really is the worst. A single sin separates us from God and that's why we need a savior.

Hear God speak:
1 Timothy 1

"This saying is trustworthy and deserving of full acceptance: "Christ Jesus came into the world to save sinners" — and I am the worst of them." (*1 Timothy 1:15 HCSB*)

My Conversation with God:

_____

_____

_____

_____

Jesus says. "... make disciples of all nations." Our assignment is simple. We are to invite others to join us in following Jesus.

Hear God speak:
Matthew 28

"Go, therefore, and make disciples of all nations, baptizing them in the name of the Father and of the Son and of the Holy Spirit, teaching them to observe everything I have commanded you. And remember, I am with you always, to the end of the age." (*Matthew 28:19-20 HCSB*)

My Conversation with God:

_____

_____

_____

_____

_____

_____

Paul's words to King Agrippa are an example. He uses a simple outline we all can use: 1) his life before becoming a follower of Jesus, 2) how he learned about or met Jesus, 3) how he chose to follow Jesus, and 4) his life since. Paul is concise. He uses his personal experience to help others choose to follow Jesus.

Every follower of Jesus can use this simple outline of their personal experience to invite someone to join them in following Jesus. It really is simple. Trust God to perform the miracle.

Hear God speak:
Acts 26

"Agrippa said to Paul, "It is permitted for you to speak for yourself." Then Paul stretched out his hand and began his defense:" (*Acts 26:1 HCSB*)

My Conversation with God:

_____

_____

The Bible records a sermon preached by Jesus. His followers heard his teachings with their own ears. You can too.

Hear God speak:
Matthew 5 - Matthew 7

"Not everyone who says to Me, 'Lord, Lord!' will enter the kingdom of heaven, but only the one who does the will of My Father in heaven. On that day many will say to Me, 'Lord, Lord, didn't we prophesy in Your name, drive out demons in Your name, and do many miracles in Your name?' Then I will announce to them, 'I never knew you! Depart from Me, you lawbreakers!'" (*Matthew 7:21-23 HCSB*)

My Conversation with God:

_____

_____

_____

_____

_____

Jesus used everyday things to explain spiritual matters. He called these stories, parables. Yet, not everybody understood.

He used familiar concepts to help us understand spiritual truths. Notice how Jesus explains these things to His followers.

Hear God speak:
Mark 4

"He would speak the word to them with many parables like these, as they were able to understand. And He did not speak to them without a parable. Privately, however, He would explain everything to His own disciples." (*Mark 4:33-34 HCSB*)

My Conversation with God:

_____

_____

_____

_____

Jesus died a horrible, painful death. He took our sin on Himself and died in our place. His death on the cross was not the end. He rose again and conquered death and the grave.

Hear God speak:
Luke 23 - Luke 24

"And Jesus called out with a loud voice, "Father, into Your hands I entrust My spirit." Saying this, He breathed His last." (*Luke 23:46 HCSB*)

"He is not here, but He has been resurrected! Remember how He spoke to you when He was still in Galilee …" (*Luke 24:6 HCSB*)

My Conversation with God:

_____

_____

_____

_____

PART SEVEN

WEEK 7

INTRODUCTION TO SEVENTH WEEK

To avoid giving up, remember, Jesus promised to finish what He started. You are not in this alone. It is about a relationship. God is at work in you and He is invested in your success.

The ultimate goal is building a deep and lasting relationship. That takes time. It is not something that is built in a single day, week, month, or even year.

Success is not measured by the number of days you can string together. It is not the sum of the parts. Relationship involves commitment and vulnerability. You will never completely arrive. It is not about a destination, it is about who you travel with along the path.

Don't be alarmed if you miss a day or two. There is an enemy and he is real. He will fight to keep you from doing what will strengthen your relationship with God.

The best news is God will never punish you for coming back. He is like the father in the story of the prodigal son. He is on the porch, anxiously watching for you to head home. He will run to meet you and embrace you. He wants to walk and talk with you.

Don't give up. You already know the joy of walking and talking with God. You know how valuable it is. It is worth your time.

It will probably help to have a plan. You know yourself and what might help. For some it is small time commitments, and others are ready for a longer plan. Either way, keep it fresh. Don't hesitate to change. You are not a slave to a system or method. You are in it for the relationship.

There are several suggestions and ideas following this final week. Now might be a good time to plan ahead. The secret is listening to God more while you talk a little less.

WEEK 7 DAY 1

Jesus began a good work in your life and He is going to finish. The creator of everything is in control. He wants even better things for you and is your companion.

Hear God speak:
Philippians 1

"I am sure of this, that He who started a good work in you will carry it on to completion until the day of Christ Jesus." (*Philippians 1:6 HCSB*)

My Conversation with God:

_____

_____

_____

_____

_____

_____

_____

Your success does not depend on you and your effort. It is God working in you that counts. The power to do, even the power to carry on, comes from Him.

Hear God speak:
Philippians 2

"Dear friends, you always followed my instructions when I was with you. And now that I am away, it is even more important. Work hard to show the results of your salvation, obeying God with deep reverence and fear. For God is working in you, giving you the desire and the power to do what pleases him." (*Philippians 2:12-13 NLT*)

My Conversation with God:

_____

_____

_____

_____

_____

WEEK 7 DAY 3

If you miss a day or two in your devotional time with God, just come back. God will be glad you did. He is always patiently waiting on you to come back. He is ready to forgive you and talk to you.

Hear God speak:
Luke 15

"So he got up and went to his father. But while the son was still a long way off, his father saw him and was filled with compassion. He ran, threw his arms around his neck, and kissed him." (*Luke 15:20 HCSB*)

My Conversation with God:

_____

_____

_____

_____

_____

WEEK 7 DAY 4

The Bible reminds us to walk and talk with God. The habit of listening to God is developed over time. Closeness is the product of time spent together.

Hear God speak:
2 Chronicles 6

"He said: Lord God of Israel, there is no God like You in heaven or on earth, keeping His gracious covenant with Your servants who walk before You with their whole heart." (*2 Chronicles 6:14 HCSB*)

My Conversation with God:

_____

_____

_____

_____

_____

_____

WEEK 7 DAY 5

Jesus uses sheep herding to illustrate His relationship with His followers because it was something people in His day would understand. His explanation is easy to understand. We are His sheep: He knows us. He calls each of us by name. And, we recognize His voice.

Hear God speak:
John 10

"But the one who enters through the gate is the shepherd of the sheep. The gatekeeper opens the gate for him, and the sheep recognize his voice and come to him. He calls his own sheep by name and leads them out. After he has gathered his own flock, he walks ahead of them, and they follow him because they know his voice." (*John 10:2-4 NLT*)

"My sheep hear My voice, I know them, and they follow Me." (*John 10:27 HCSB*)

My Conversation with God:

_____

_____

The key to consistency is to not give up. God is at work in you. If you have made it this far, you have enough days to have a habit. It is a good rhythm to have.

Hear God speak:
2 Corinthians 4
1 John 1:9

"Therefore we do not give up. Even though our outer person is being destroyed, our inner person is being renewed day by day." (*2 Corinthians 4:16 HCSB*)

"If we confess our sins, He is faithful and righteous to forgive us our sins and to cleanse us from all unrighteousness." (*1 John 1:9 HCSB*)

My Conversation with God:

_____

_____

_____

_____

Your primary motivation to keep going is to remember you are in a relationship with God. The creator of the universe is talking to you. Don't forget, Jesus is coming back.

Hear God speak:
Revelation 22

"He who testifies about these things says, 'Yes, I am coming quickly.' Amen! Come, Lord Jesus!" (*Revelation 22:20 HCSB*)

My Conversation with God:

_____

_____

_____

_____

_____

_____

_____

PART EIGHT

FOLLOW THROUGH

NEXT STEPS

Find Time To Review

If you have made it this far set aside a time to reread your entries. What did God Say? What did you say?

It may require more than a single day. Start by asking God to show you a more complete picture of what He has been doing.

You may want to mark key words or thoughts. You may want to use another page. If you like diagrams or drawings as better ways to express yourself, do what comes natural to you. God made you that way so he will understand perfectly. Look for themes or patterns. For example, jot down a list of keywords.

If those ideas don't fit you, adapt. Sometimes we only see part of what God is saying as we are going through the daily grind. You are wanting to hear from the one who made you; it won't be hard. God is not trying to be mysterious. He wants you to get the message.

Remember, God wants a deeper relationship with you and a conversation is vital to that depth. Stop and take time to listen. Only you and God know what it is really about.

Some have found a personal retreat helpful. An occasional half day or longer might work for you. You do not need to spend extra money on a location. Anyplace that offers uninterrupted time and space can work.

If you are a visual person, a vantage point that allows you to see or visualize the city, town, or community God has called you to reach might be appropriate. A map may be a way God uses. It could be as simple as an empty conference room or a second story window. The place and the fixtures are not really important. You are setting aside time to spend listening to God. Just ask Him where He wants to meet you.

Bible Reading Plans

Structure is only valuable if it gets you to the objective. The purpose is simple: listen to God more while you practice having a conversation.

Remember the purpose of Bible reading is to hear God speak. Be careful not to rush. It is usually better to start small. I often had to pause and reflect, even in the middle of a verse, in order to hear what God was saying to me. Slow and deliberate reading may help you process what God is saying. Don't be afraid to suspend your reading to ask God to help you.

Read five Psalms and one chapter of Proverbs each day. This will allow you to read both books in one month (31 days). Billy Graham pointed out, "One half of all the quotes that Jesus made from the Old Testament came from the book of Psalms, because the psalmist lived every experience that we live. He was up one day and down the next. He had every kind of thought. Then he would talk to God about it."

Read the story of Jesus. Matthew, Mark, Luke and John are called the gospels. Read a few verses (a complete story) or a chapter.

Use Bible apps or books. Keep the focus on God's Word.

This is not the time to hear what great women or men of God have to say. In other words, devotionals (even short ones) may actually keep you from hearing God. The Bible is always the safest option.

Beware of reading plans that are too ambitious for you. Simple is sometimes better.

If you listen or learn better by hearing, find an app that will play recordings of the Bible. Even those who read well might benefit from listening for a time.

Design your own plan. Remember to focus on listening to God speak through the Bible.

A Written Record

Blank pages usually work best. Any format will do. A spiral bound notebook, a three ring binder, a permanently bound notebook or any other pages will do fine.

If investing in an expensive bound notebook helps you value the investment more and helps you be more consistent, do it. But remember, the price does not determine the value. You usually get out in proportion to the effort you put in, not the money.

Format

The system or format that works for you is the best system.

I keep it simple. The date, the Bible reference or references, and a few lines of what I said to God are the essentials for me.

Don't be afraid to change something. You can always go back to something that worked before. But, remember the wise saying, "If it ain't broke, don't fix it."

Confidentiality

Guard confidentiality carefully. I always assumed what I wrote might be read by someone else. Therefore, I never included anything that I would not want shouted from the rooftop.

There were times when I intentionally wrote in a way that God and I would only know. For example, I might write, "Help me forgive the person you and I know I need to forgive." or "Show me how to talk to the person you and I know I need to talk to. You know what I need to talk to them about and why that is hard for me." or "You know what is on my heart today. Help me." These example, and other like them, keep confidential matters between me and God. He knows my thoughts and I am not hiding anything from Him.

Pass It On

If God is teaching you, He wants you to pass it on.

The best way to really learn something well is to teach it to someone else. If God is teaching you something helpful, ask Him to show you who to share it with. You don't need to have the title "teacher", you just have to let God use you. Remember, it is His idea.

Encouragement

If God is at work in your life, don't keep it to yourself. Tell somebody! It is worth celebrating. If you want, write me and tell me what God is doing in your life.

Email me at:ronnie@BeyondMyStrength.com

ABOUT THE AUTHOR

Ronnie Fox is a writer and minister living in Cumming, Georgia. He is married to Gwenn. They have three adult children and three grandsons.

His ministry experience includes six years as a member of the Church Planting Group at the North American Mission Board, SBC. In this ministry, he served as a strategic coordinator for starting churches in urban centers across the U.S. and Canada.

Ronnie and Gwenn also served as missionaries assigned to Peru with the International Mission Board, SBC, from February 1986 until August 2004. These 18 years of ministry included a variety of roles among Spanish-speaking and Quechua-speaking Peruvians.

He is currently disabled due to a stroke he suffered in August 2010 that left him partially paralyzed on his right side. In November of 2012, Ronnie formed Fox Ministries, Inc.

For more information see:
BeyondMyStrength.com

Contact Ronnie at:
ronnie@BeyondMyStrength.com

BASED ON THE BOOK

Beyond My Strength

by Ronnie Fox

BeyondMyStrength.com
See inside the book on Amazon

Made in the USA
Middletown, DE
28 September 2021